Kid's Guide to Helping the Planet

For Kids, By Kids

BY KAI BROWN

TABLE OF CONTENTS

THIS BOOK IS DEDICATED TO THIS PLACE WE CALL HOME AND
THOSE WHO FIND WONDER IN IT

VISIT US AT:

https://kidshelpingtheplanet.com/

INTRODUCTION

Hello Esteemed Readers! If you're reading this, it means that you care about the planet... I hope, or possibly, your parents are forcing you to learn about Climate Change... either way, I'm excited that you're here! My name is Kai Brown and I'm glad you're interested in learning more about this place we call home. I'm currently fifteen years old and I'm trying my best to understand and help the planet. I believe the little things can make a big difference. I try my best to recycle, compost, save electricity, and avoid using large amounts of non-renewable resources. It also means I advocate with my parents to make better decisions within our community.

The main reasons I'm writing this book are to increase awareness about how we are harming the environment, to share ideas on how to help, and to raise money for organizations that are out there solving major problems—like air and water pollution, Climate Change, deforestation, adaptation solutions, and more. The hope is to educate people about our planet and demonstrate that our small, day-to-day choices can change the world. I'm also writing to say there is hope for the future. Everyday we're making progress toward more conscious decisions about our planet. The advancements in technology are exciting. People around the global continue to innovate to address issues like Climate Change. There are two key things I've learned about the choices we can make to help the environment. The first is that no choice is too small. I've also learned that one person isn't enough to save the world—this takes a collective effort.

This book is hopefully an educational and fun experience. I've included interesting anecdotes, statistics, and compelling facts. For example, did you know the United States goes through **100 billion** plastic bags a year?

There is much debate about our planet amongst scientists and politicians but given the rigor in the scientific community and the tremendous amounts of data collected, this book will approach these issues from a scientific perspective. No matter what you believe personally, it's clear that our planet is changing and we're contributing to that change without understanding all the consequences.

This book covers the problems affecting the world around you and ways to make a healthy impact on the planet. I'll discuss the current condition of our planet and what scientists believe is happening. I'll talk about things

6

you, even as kids, can do to make a difference in your home and community. I'll share some of the big problems. Sometimes these problems seem too large to fix as an individual but starting smaller in scope and focusing on your home and local community is a great way to help.

This book covers some regional areas on the planet tainted by humans, like large masses of garbage in the Pacific Ocean. In addition, there will be a list projects and organizations that help the environment and that are looking for support from people like you. Since I'm from Washington State, I'll touch on some of the history in my area.

In my life, I've learned that there is a myriad of ways to lower my carbon footprint, increase recycling effects, and utilize renewable energy and materials. When reading this book, keep an eye out for Planet Hacks and Tips along the way. I hope that this book helps educate you about the planet, and makes you feel like you are part of our global community as well!

If we all do our part in preserving our home, we can create a bright future for new generations and ourselves.

I appreciate your support. *100% of all proceeds from this book and t-shirt sales will go towards programs aimed at helping the environment and preserving the planet.*

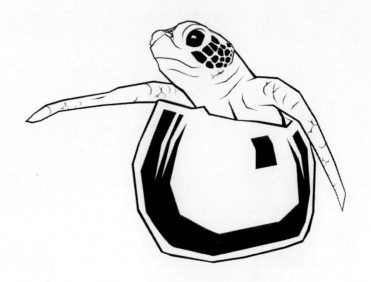

CHAPTER ONE

WHY SHOULD I CARE ABOUT THE PLANET?

To some, this may seem like a silly question, but it's important. One of the primary challenges in helping the planet is getting people to believe there is a problem. Once people truly believe there is a problem, the next challenge is convincing them to take meaningful action. This is especially difficult when the problem seems so large, incentives aren't always aligned, we are constantly learning new information scientifically, and there are political debates about the matter.

My reason for helping the environment is so I can keep our planet safe for my family and future generations. I also personally want to keep the planet safe for all the animals and plants with which we cohabitate. I even have specific species that are near and dear to my heart. Many of these animals are in trouble because of the pollution, deforestation, or Climate Change.

I care about the sea life in the ocean dearly because of an experience I had when I was ten years old. My family was on vacation in Mexico for summer break. Two other families travelled with us to enjoy the time off. We stayed near the beach. The parents were relaxing while we kids played in the pool.

One day, I was in the swimming pool with one of my closest friends. While we were playing, I heard a splashing noise behind me. Normally, I wouldn't have given it a second thought. However, I hadn't heard anyone behind me playing previously. Curious about the mysterious source of the noise, I turned around to see a small piece of what I believed was driftwood in the pool.

"That's odd," I thought, "Where would that have come from?"

Upon closer inspection, I realized it was moving! It wasn't driftwood at all... it was a baby sea turtle.

"How did it get here?" I wondered. My dad came over and informed me that the turtle fell into the pool from the mouth of a seagull that flew overhead. The ocean was less than thirty yards away, so we picked it up and started carrying it down to the beach.

I'd never held a baby turtle before. It was so tiny and adorable, and it was the first creature I'd been able to rescue. We dropped it back into the ocean while tearfully saying goodbye. It dove into the water. We all stood there and watched it swim away with a sense of joy. It looked so small relative to the vast environment into which it ventured. I thought it was going to live a long and happy life... at least I hoped.

We talked about the turtle for the rest of the trip and well beyond. My parents purchased a souvenir for me to remind us of the event, you can see it below:

This moment in my life created a profound connection for me with the living creatures around us. I've learned more recently that these very sea turtles are in danger of extinction due to Climate Change. A personal reason for writing this book is to help preserve these precious creatures.

So why should **you** care?

A big reason people should care is because the planet is our home and we're unlikely to have another one anytime soon. For many, these problems seem far away, but if you could imagine shrinking these problems down to a single farm, they might seem more understandable.

Planet Fact

According to NASA, Earth's atmosphere is composed of 78% nitrogen, 21% oxygen, 0.04% carbon dioxide, and trace amounts of neon, helium, methane, krypton and hydrogen, as well as water vapor.

Let's imagine you lived on a farm, let's call it Farm Earth.

On Farm Earth, there are chickens that provide eggs, plants that produce fruits and vegetables, crystal-clear rivers full of fish and other aquatic life, and a lush landscape full of trees. It has a delicate balance within this stately environment. However, people come to your farm and begin committing atrocities. Okay, atrocities may be a bit much, but people start to show up and influence your farm in negative ways.

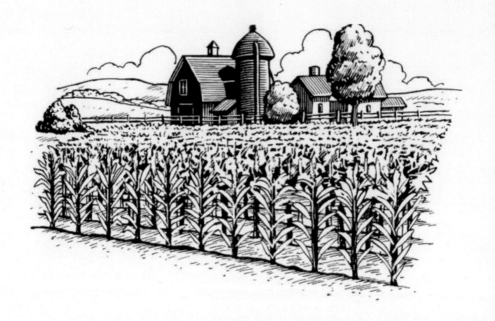

First, they start to take more chickens than you can produce. They've taken your chickens because of the demand for food outside the farm. Over time, you are slowly running out of chickens, a valuable element in your environment, and you're unable to nourish your family properly.

At the farm, chickens produce food and waste. Both are beneficial to the functioning's of the farm. The food is a source of nutrients for you and your family, and the waste is a source of nutrients for plants and crops. Now that you've lost your chickens, Farm Earth lacks food to eat and a fundamental element that aids other vital organisms like plants.

Next, people start chopping down trees and other plants to make space for a factory uphill from your farm. Trees serve myriad key purposes that stabilizes the environment from disasters such as mudslides, floods, or soil erosion. Now that people have cut down the trees surrounding your

12

property, there is a danger of floods that could originate from the river or other water sources. The would-be, firmly packed soil seeps water, which creates a surplus of water on the surface. When people cut down trees, Farm Earth will be partially flooded, which has meaningful ramifications to ongoing operations.

The factory uphill starts to dump garbage on your land, which reduces the amount of land you're able to use for farming. This puts even more pressure on providing food to your family. Pollutants from the factory are making people in your family sick and less safe to drink the water. Those same pollutants are affecting the animals and getting into the food your family eats. This increases the cost of keeping people healthy.

Now add to this that the emissions from the factories are impacting weather patterns, health of crops, amount of water and fish in the rivers, wildlife in on the farm, and much more. The emissions are increasing temperatures, putting additional pressure on the ability to grow healthy crops and contributing to rising river levels. These factors increase mounting pressure that make it difficult for you to maintain your farm.

In many ways, our planet is suffering like Farm Earth—but the effects are often hidden from your day-to-day life. If these effects were happening in your backyard, you might have a great sense of urgency. There are many problems facing our planet, but most seem fixable if we do our part.

Planet Hack

Avoid single-use plastics. The U.N. reports that just 9% of the world's 9 billion tons of plastic have been recycled. According to the U.N., the most commonly single-use plastics are:

- Plastic drinking bottles
- Plastic bottle caps
- Food wrappers
- Plastic grocery bags
- Plastic lids
- Straws and stirrers

CHAPTER TWO

HOW IS THE PLANET DOING?

Fortunately, the planet is in no danger of exploding anytime soon! However, many scientists have been sounding the alarm that the planet is in danger of significant changes faster than previously thought. In this chapter, I'll be covering the key issues affecting our planet, like Climate Change – one of the biggest problems facing our generation. There are several key issues affecting the environment, which include:

- **Climate Change**
- **Pollution**
- **Deforestation/Wildfires**
- **Species Extinction/Overfishing**
- **Soil Degradation**

Below is a quick summary of each issue before we dive deeper into specifics.

Climate Change

Climate Change is the first topic we will be covering. This also happens to be one of the biggest and most controversial. Climate Change is a change in global or regional climate patterns. Scientist believe Climate Changes have accelerated because of the large use of fossil fuels in the late 20th century.

Fossil fuels are natural fuels formed in the geological past from the remains of living organisms such as: plants, dinosaurs, and smaller organisms. That's why they are **fossil** fuels.

One of the problems with fossil fuels is they are not renewable, as they take a very long time to form. Remember that almost all known plants and animals get their energy from the sun. Therefore, fossil fuel is really sun energy that has been stored in the ground over millions of years.

Now, imagine in a short period, we're unlocking all that energy and emissions into Earth's atmosphere at a rate never done before. Scientists say this affects the environment by changing the general temperature of the planet.

Before we get much further, we should introduce a little molecule called Carbon Dioxide, which forms when we burn fossil fuels—along with other greenhouse gases. I know, sounds fancy, but it is quite simple. One carbon atom and two oxygen atoms that are connected:

Carbon Dioxide (commonly known as CO2)

We use fossil fuels—which emit carbon dioxide—for energy to power our houses, move our vehicles, produce the food we eat, manufacture products, and for other common uses.

 *Planet Tip*

It is clear from extensive scientific evidence that the dominant cause of the rapid change in climate of the past half century is human-induced increases in the amount of atmospheric greenhouse gases, including carbon dioxide.

NASA used ice cores to create the model below to show the amount of carbon dioxide in the atmosphere dating back to over 400,000 years ago. In other words, they use pieces of air in ice to tell what was in the air at different times. With these bubbles of air, scientists can put together the following spike in carbon dioxide levels:

17

http://climatechange12.com/01pics/nasa-climate-change.jpg

Pollution

Pollution is next up! For those of you who live in the United States, **40%** of people are living in areas with unhealthy levels of air pollution. This worldwide problem is due to several factors: burning of fossil fuels, agricultural activity, indoor pollutants, and more.

Unfortunately, activities that contribute to air pollution also contribute to respiratory and heart problems in humans. Just like humans, animals suffer from the negative affected by pollutants as well.

Deforestation

Deforestation is the act of destroying or removing a group of trees then using that same area for non-forest use. Clear-cutting, which is cutting down large areas of tree at once, and burning trees are the most common methods of deforestation. This is a large problem because without trees to hold the ground steady we could have soil erosion and flooding, which could destroy the homelands of the indigenous people living in the Amazon or other forest inhabitants and could harm us as well. Tree also convert carbon dioxide into oxygen, so with fewer trees, the more our environment produced more greenhouse gases.

Species Extinction/Overfishing

In the US, over 3,000 species of animals are considered endangered. Even after the Endangered Species Act passed in 1973, there are now three times as many endangered species from just ten years ago. Overfishing is the act of fishing a species of fish at a rate in which it cannot replenish its population. In other words, species are dying, and fish are disappearing from the oceans of the world at an alarming rate. As protections roll back for many species and Climate Change is applying increasing pressure, many creatures are in danger of extinction.

Soil Degradation

Soil degradation is the decline in soil quality due to improper land use for agriculture, urban, or industrial purposes. The main areas of concern are soil acidity problems, bad internal drainage, and low organic matter in the soil. This can stop the growth of plants and affect the survival of animals that rely on the flora.

Summary

These problems are currently affecting the world around us. There are other potential problems that I have not listed, but this is a good start. We'll dive deeper into some of these topics and talk about ways to solve the problems that affect our planet.

CHAPTER THREE

MAKING AN IMPACT STARTS AT HOME

What can one do to make an impact? This may surprise you, but your family makes an impact every day. By driving a car that runs with gasoline, or even electricity, you are making an impact. This happens because of the use of resources such as water, electricity, fossil fuels, food, and chemicals.

This maybe a negative or positive impact but this chapter will be about a few easy ways to make a positive impact on the environment by saving your resources in daily life. There are options that may not be as practical for your family, like installing solar panels, but there are some easy ways to make a positive impact at home by adhering to the following strategies.

An important resource to save and use economically is electricity as it mainly comes from fossil fuels. An easy way to save electricity is to completely turnoff equipment like televisions, stereos, and lights when you're not using them. This habit is a small choice but sometimes I forget. Also advocating with your parents to use energy efficient light bulbs. LED light bulbs use 75%-80% less energy than traditional light bulbs, now that's a bright idea!

Another way to lower your electricity use is to lower your shades or close your curtains on hot days. This way you will keep the house cool and reduce the use of electric fans or air-conditioning by blocking the sun. This will save a mammoth amount of energy because heating and cooling consumes nearly half of a home's energy.

Keeping lids on pans when cooking is a way to conserve energy and lower the amount of fossil fuels used yearly. Some other easy ways to save electricity are to avoid opening the refrigerator for extending periods of time. Also, you can buy energy-efficient appliances to cut down the need for electricity. For example, an advanced power strip is like a normal power strip but keeps idle electronics from drawing energy from the power grid or house. Electricity is essential for living comfortably, but there are simple ways to reduce your energy use to save money, and to improve your home's sustainability.

Like electricity, we have many other resources that come from our Earth that we need to preserve, such as water. Saving water is a great way to help the environment. As Americans, we waste over seven billion gallons of water annually. To save water, you can take some simple steps. Like remembering to turn off the tap when you are brushing your teeth or shaving. Or you can try to collect the water used to wash vegetables and salad to water your houseplants. Another way to avoid wasting water is to use water appliances appropriately. This saving method applies to washing machines and dishwashers. When using a washing machine or a dishwasher, we should to try to avoid using these machines unless they are almost or completely full. Shorter showers are another great way to use less water.

Another way is to use rechargeable batteries, this way you can save money and help the environment. By using rechargeable, you are reducing the CO_2 emissions by lowering the amount of resources needed to move the batteries and to create them. By using rechargeable batteries, battery providers do not need to use as many resources for production and transportation.

Even if you do not plan to buy rechargeable batteries, you can recycle the batteries because the industry that makes batteries is a closed cycle. When you recycle old batteries, you create less of a demand of new materials for building new technology: computers and electronic devices. When batteries arrive at the landfills, most of them can release harmful metals such as mercury, lead, cadmium into the environment.

By using rechargeable batteries, you will be limiting the number of non-biodegradables in our landfills. In other words, if you recycle all the batteries the manufactures won't have to use other materials from the Earth that could be used for other jobs while leaving space for other waste in landfills. So, we can use the empty space for non-degradable like plastic and chemicals.

Another way is avoiding single-use products like plastic plates or plastic knives, forks, and cups. This way plastic is used less, and more things can be recycled. I find this one a little hard for events because it can be hard to carry around during large events, parties, or just catching up with people. Sending electronic greeting cards over email, instead of paper cards, to lower the need of paper which lowers the need to cut trees down and burn fossil fuels to deliver mail.

Another way is to get green energy for electricity instead of from fossil fuels. This is called **Green Pricing**. This allows you to pay a small fee in exchange for electricity generated from clean, renewable (green) energy sources. This eliminates the need for the 14 barrels of oils to power the electricity of a person, but instead we can fund green energy for our own use and other's as well.

 Planet Hack

In some areas, you can pay a little extra money on your electrical bill to use renewable energy like solar, wind, and hydroelectric. This increases demand for green energy and accelerate its use. Encouraging your parents to change your electrical bill to green energy will decrease the demand for fossil fuels.

Technology is helping us as well. There are tools and applications to help understand your energy usage to figure out your largest areas of usage. Once you know where your family is using the most energy and resources, it is easier fix those problem areas. Even if you don't have the ability to install these tools, look at your families next utility bill to familiarize yourself with how your family consumes energy.

Another major way to help the planet is to take public transportation instead of driving your family car everywhere. Transportation is a major contributor to the burning of fossil fuels.

All these choices affect the world around you and your consumption of resources. By following some of these tips from each topic, you will be able to limit the use of fossil, single-use products, and the waste in our landfill and conserve key resources like electricity, energy, and water. Applying all these choices to your life is difficult but if you apply just a few, or few at a time, it will reduce your negative impact on the environment. Making changes at your home really makes a difference.

CHAPTER FIVE

CLIMATE CHANGE

We've discussed Climate Change briefly in previous chapters, but it deserves a full chapter for us to dive in deeper on the subject. We'll revisit fossil fuels, global warming, greenhouse gases, and much more. In my opinion, this is the most important topic when discussing helping the planet and protecting future generations. Although the climate is generally changing, it is changing at rates previously never seen and we don't fulling understand all the ramifications. Discussing what we do know will hopefully give a better understanding of this important issue. Okay! It's Explanation Time!

Global warming is an increase in the average global temperature caused primarily by the increase of greenhouse gases trapped in our atmosphere. Greenhouse gases are gases that trap heat. This means that the more greenhouse gases there are—like nitrous oxide, carbon dioxide, and methane—the more the Earth heats up. This was called global warming until scientists realized that the temperature is becoming colder and hotter. Then, scientists began to call it Climate Change because it was not only getting hotter but colder in areas.

 ## *Planet Fact*

Did you know Venus is the hottest planet in the solar system at 462 degrees Celsius primarily because of runaway greenhouse gas effects? Scientist have already seen the effects of greenhouse gases on other planets in our own solar system.

The average temperature has been rising more than it has fallen and although the earth's climate fluctuates, the temperature hasn't reached todays levels in over the last four hundred thousand years or more. This problem mostly began around the 1760s. In other words, Climate Change was very likely caused by the industrial revolution.

The Industrial Revolution started in the 1760s where machines—instead of human energy—use energy from fossil fuels, like oil and coal (the stuff Santa gives to kids that are on the naughty list).

During the Industrial Revolution there was massive population growth and huge increases in consumption of energy around the world. It did a lot to help increase the quality of life for people but set the stage for damaging the planet in ways we hadn't anticipated.

When the Industrial Revolution started, people used three main types of energy:

COAL   OIL   NATURAL GAS

Basically, over a couple hundred years, we've released a lot of carbon dioxide and other greenhouse gases and those gases have trapped heat from the sun, which is hurting the planet. The amount of greenhouse gases emitted into our environment is staggering.

The anticipated effects of Climate Change are broad reaching This includes impacts to food, health, oceans, weather, and more. An example that we are witnessing now is that glaciers and ice sheets in Greenland and Antarctica are melting at an alarming rate. NASA monitors the state of these areas and it is clear through satellite imagery that they are changing. This run off is increasing sea levels around the world.

So why does Carbon Dioxide get all the attention? Amongst the greenhouse gases, it's like the popular kid at school. The reason carbon dioxide is the most problematic greenhouse gas is because there is so much more of it dumped in the atmosphere

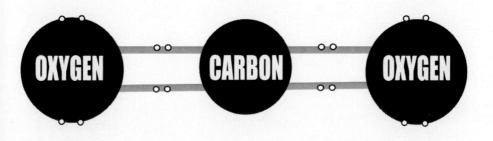

.

 *Planet Fact*

Did you know that we breathe out Carbon Dioxide? We exhaled approximately two and a half pounds of Carbon Dioxide a day.

Climate Change has and will to continue damage the environment. An example of this damage is one of my favorite trees. Let me tell you a quick story about a trip I took when I was younger.

Three years ago, I went to Joshua Tree National Park after doing a school project about the park. I got to see one of the weirdest trees and rock formations I had ever seen, and the entire park was filled with different animals and plants. The variety of the plants was astoundingly majestic. One of these amazing plants was the Joshua tree.

The Joshua tree, also known as a yucca palm, is an evergreen plant that belongs to the lily family. There are actually three subspecies that are found in the Mojave Desert. These unique looking trees can grow to 15 to 40 feet tall. I got to see this special tree up close. It was definitely one of a kind.

(Pictures of Joshua tree)

Sadly, if the global temperature continues to raise, there is a real chance that these trees could go extinct by 2070.

To help you understand the problem of Climate Change, the contributors of greenhouse gases today are primarily electricity, transportation, and industry. You can see the percentages from the graph below:

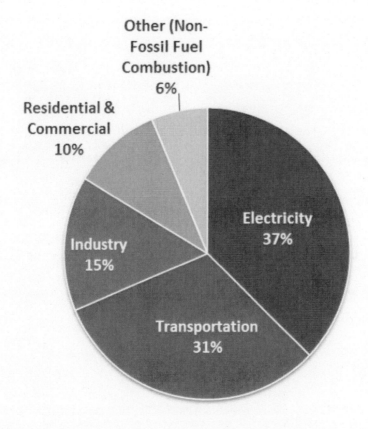

Planet Fact

Did you know Washington State produces approximately 60% of its energy from renewable sources, such as hydroelectric power? However, portions of this energy are "exported" to other states and we actually consume approximately 60% of our energy from large amounts of coal burning in Montana. So, when we plug in our electric vehicles, we're charging with 60% coal power unless we specify otherwise on our electric bill. Interesting, huh?

To ensure a stable and healthy environment for future generations, we should advocate for stabilizing Climate Change. Although Climate Change is the biggest issue, it isn't the only challenge we face when it comes to helping the planet.

"I blame entropy."

CHAPTER SIX

POLLUTION

It's hard enough keeping my room clean! Imagine having to deal with keeping an entire planet clean. Pollution comes in many forms and affects the environment in different ways. Fortunately, there are organizations and regulations to help protect everyone. That being said, there are still plenty of problems that exist due to people and companies polluting the planet. Part of that pollution makes it back into our bodies through the air we breathe and the water we drink. This is causing us health issues, including shortened life spans. We'll focus on air pollution and water pollution in this chapter as these two pose some of the most challenging problems for people.

WATER POLLUTION

Water pollution is when pollutants, such as garage or chemicals, enter bodies of water like lakes, rivers, seas, oceans, and groundwater. This occurs when the pollutants enter the water without proper treatment or filtering. Surprisingly, agriculture is one of the major sources of water pollution because the fertilizers to feed the crops wash into the lakes and rivers. Let me give you a little history about one of the prominent lakes in my area.

Lake Washington

Lake Washington is an 18-mile-long lake next to Seattle, Washington. The lake's width varies from two to six miles covering an area of 34 square miles. This is a final resting place for about one hundred boats, fifty planes, a coal train, and other odd objects that sank over the years. Lake Washington has been a dumping ground for about 150 years.

This disastrous practice exists around the world and can severely harm the environment and its animals and plants on lands as well as in water. In the 1960s, the blue-algae flourished from the pollution and washed up on the shores, earning the lake the name "Lake Stinko" by the local papers. By the 1970s, Lake Washington achieved a healthy level of clarity as pollutant and algae levels declined. By the 1990s, the clarity and cleanliness of the lake was as good as it had been prior to industrialization thanks to local efforts.

All cities get dirty. The lesson from Lake Washington is whether the city takes cleaning efforts seriously or not.

China Chemical Leaks

In 2013, a chemical accident leaked a chemical compound called benzene, a known cancer-causing agent, into a branch of the Huangpu River in China. Benzene is very harmful to the body when people are exposed to it for a long amount of time. This caused thousands of pigs to die and float past Shanghai. In this accident, more than 20 people were hospitalized as a result and area residents were forced to rely on fire trucks to provide safe drinking water. Dramatic, and messed up as this is, they may be the least of China's water pollution worries.

These people in this accident are not the only people with water pollution issues. The Economist reports that more than half of China's surface water is so polluted it cannot be treated to make it drinkable, and one-quarter of it is so dangerous it can't even be used for industrial purposes.

Sadly, groundwater isn't any safer. About 40 percent of China's farmland depends on underground water for irrigation, and an estimated 90 percent is polluted, Reuters (a news site) reports. The groundwater under Chinese cities has gotten so bad that 60 percent of it has been deemed "severely polluted" by the Economist.

China's environmental problems seem to spring up on a scale as broad and epic as the large nation itself. But China's increasingly restive population of 1.3 billion people is now starting to demand government action to combat the deadly threats of pollution and disease. However, Chinese officials have hardly began to acknowledge the problem. In the meantime, the people of China are forced to deal with these environmental catastrophes in their day-to-day life.

Great Pacific Garbage Patch

The Great Pacific Garbage Patch is a massive swirling pile of trash in the Pacific Ocean. This is a topic I heard about when I was younger. If this problem was recognized as a Texas-sized problem, it might be solved by now, right? Sadly, I am sorry to say that this colossal problem is not improving. In fact, it seems to be growing faster than scientists have expected, and no one knows the exact size. When I was a kid, the Pacific Garbage Patch was roughly the size of the state of Texas. Now, it is estimated to be two to three times bigger.

So how was the Garbage Patch discovered?

Well, once upon a twenty-or-so years ago in 1997, the Great Pacific Garbage Patch was discovered by a man named Charles Moore. He discovered "Moore" than he bargained for that day.

Captain Moore founded the Algalita Foundation and commanded its research ship, the Alguita. Moore first discovered the Pacific Garbage Patch when he crossed the Pacific in 1997 after competing in the Transpacific Yacht Race. I can just imagine the competitors talking strategy. "Oh George! The Duke of Wellington has taken the upper hand. Should we speed up? George:

Preposterous! We could spill our cocktail." Yeah, I feel like it wasn't that competitive of a race. Okay moving along.

Since Charles Moore found the Garbage Patch, he has been passionate about investigating it and creating awareness about its significance. His discovery has gone a long way toward educating the science community and the public of the magnitude that this pollution is having on marine life.

AIR POLLUTION

Air pollution is when substances are released into the air that have harmful or poisonous effects. Air pollution in Beijing is so bad that the U.S. Embassy's air quality measuring station can only call it "beyond index." Ha! It's like my breath in the morning... *cough* Seriously though, air pollution is considered the top environmental killer contributing to an estimated 3.5 million deaths a year. Two of the biggest countries that deal with poor air quality are China and India.

China

In China, there are Industrial towns where rates of cancer are so high, they're known as "cancer villages." Along with these frightening problems, the Chinese government is silent about anything that might disrupt the country's economic development—including environmental regulation.

Manufacturing industries and Beijing's 5 million-plus cars all contribute to the city's crippling air pollution, but many blame the coal-burning electrical plants that power China's breakneck economic growth. According to the New York Times, China now burns a whopping 47 percent of the world's coal, roughly equal to the amount used by all other countries of the world combined. Unfortunately, a large network of coal-burning power plants surrounds the city of Beijing.

But as polluted as it is, Beijing's air isn't even China's worst: That horrific honor goes to Ürümqi in China's far west side. Ürümqi has recently joined the other Chinese cities like Lanzhou and Linfen on lists of the world's most polluted places.

Summary

Like I said, pollution comes in many forms, but you can help based on the products you purchase, the modes of transportation you choose, the politicians you support, recycling and reuse, and the steps you take to help Climate Change. Let's all support a clean and healthy planet.

INTERESTING FACTS & STATISTICS

There is a bunch of great information about helping the planet in other books. This chapter talks about some interesting facts related to the environment that you might not already know. These facts are important because these statistics can encourage people to learn more about the problems around them.

(http://www.who.int/topics/environmental_health/factsheets/en/)

Daily, we use 10 billion tons of freshwater around the world.

The planet's average surface temperature has increased by 1.62 F degrees since the late 19th century

An average of 281 billion tons of ice per year melted between 1993 and 2016

Global sea levels rose about 8 inches in the last century, the rate has double from last century

The rate of acidity of surface water has grown to 30 percent

4 million people prematurely died from illnesses attributable to household air pollution from inefficient cooking practices using polluting stoves paired with solid fuels and kerosene.

45% of all pneumonia deaths in children less than 5 years old are caused by exposure to household air pollution

In 2015, only 71% of the global population (5.2 billion) used a safely managed drinking-water service.

2.47 million trees are cut down a day

2.1 billion people globally lack safe water at home.

Of those 2.1 billion people, 263 million spend more than 30 minutes per round trip collecting water.

159 million drink water directly from surface sources, such as streams or lakes.

844 million do not have basic drinking water services.

By 2025, half the world will be living in water-stressed areas

Between 2030 and 2050, Climate Change is expected to cause approximately 250,000 additional deaths per year

With extreme heat proves to be difficult leading to 70,000 excess deaths in 2003 in Europe

Globally, the reported number of reported weather-related natural disasters has more than tripled since 1960 resulting in a yearly toll of 60,000 deaths.

27% of the world (1.9 billion) used private sanitation facilities connected to sewers where the wastewater maybe treated

2.3 billion people don't have basic sanitation facilities

13% of the global population (0.9 billion) used toilets or latrines

CHAPTER SEVEN

TALKING WITH AN EXPERT

Sometimes it's better to hear directly from an expert instead of a teen like myself. I had the opportunity to interview a climate expert from the Climate Impacts Group focused on the Pacific Northwest region. It's a fascinating interview and I learned a lot about his work. You can see the interview below:

Guillaume Mauger, Ph.D.
Research scientist, Climate Impacts Group

Expertise: Pacific Northwest Climate Change and effects on temperature, precipitation, and sea level.

Question:

Can you give me a little background on how you're helping the planet?

Answer:

I work with the Climate Impacts Group. Generally, Climate Change initiatives fall into two camps: Mitigation and Adaptation. Mitigation focuses on reducing greenhouse gas emissions. Adaptation has nothing to do with reducing greenhouse gases, but prepares for changes that are coming our way, because we're clearly not going to reduce all the affects over the years.

My work is focused on Adaptation. The reason I work at the Climate Impacts Group is to work to integrate the science with the practice of Climate Change. We work with the state, state agencies, federal agencies, and tribes to help them prepare for Climate Change and how they are currently, and will be, impacted.

My work is focused on flooding, sea level rise, rivers, and more.

Question:

What do you anticipate will happen to temperatures and sea levels in the Pacific Northwest?

Answer:

I believe we're going to see bigger changes over the next century. We're most confident in the changes we'll see in water levels like sea level and rivers. The report we published includes absolute sea level rise projections, in feet, for Washington State:

PROJECTED ABSOLUTE SEA LEVEL CHANGE
(feet, averaged over each 19-year time period)

Time Period	Greenhouse Gas Scenario	Central Estimate (50%)	Likely[5] Range (83-17%)	Higher magnitude, but lower likelihood possibilities		
				10% probability of exceedance	1% probability of exceedance	0.1% probability of exceedance
2050 (2040-2059)	Low	0.6	0.4 - 0.8	0.9	1.2	1.8
	High	0.7	0.5 - 0.9	1.0	1.3	2.0
2100 (2090-2109)	Low	1.6	1.0 - 2.2	2.5	4.1	7.2
	High	2.0	1.4 - 2.8	3.1	4.8	8.3
2150 (2140-2159)	Low	2.5	1.5 - 3.8	4.4	8.5	16.2
	High	3.4	2.3 - 4.9	5.6	10.0	18.3

(https://cig.uw.edu/wp-content/uploads/sites/2/2019/07/SLR-Report-Miller-et-al-2018-updated-07_2019.pdf)

Question:

Do you believe enough is being done to fight Climate Change?

Answer:

No, I don't. That's not a surprising answer. We have small fact sheets we put out. There are consequences about pulling back emissions. We're not doing enough, and we're on a trajectory that within a year we'll have made it impossible to stick to the one-and-a-half-degree target. The anticipated impact is massive.

I was looking at the changes in Tacoma in the Puyallup river for flooding, that 100-year flood is going to double by the end of the century and it's already a huge amount of water.

Where you're going to see the biggest changes are the rivers where you have a lot of snow upstream.

Questions:

What do you think is the most effective way for young people to help?

Answer:

I think the most important way to help is that it's not enough to just be informed and vote and read the right articles, I think you must do something. People disparage things like changing light bulbs, composting your food, becoming vegetarian, but these are important things to do. I think being involved in the political process as much as possible. Whether at the city, state, or international level. As a young person, you have more of a voice than I do.

Question:

As you've learned about the environment around you, what have you found most surprising?

Answer:

One of the things that has been surprising to me, since I look at rivers and water in the region, even before Climate Change was something people thought about, we've done a lot as people to alter our water systems.

It's really striking how these systems have been altered by humans. I work with a biologist that believes if we undid some of the changes we've made, many of the fish would be fine with Climate Change.

Many rivers have been straightened to help with flooding and boating and they have built up floodplains, but these changes have fundamentally altered the environment. There is a lot of potential to restore things to their natural state.

I would also say there are ways to adapting to Climate Changes that may make Climate Change seem invisible. Humans adapt to all kinds of harsh and unfriendly circumstances and we have short memories.

Question:

What gives you the most hope around efforts to fight Climate Change?

Answer:

That's a hard one. It's hard because there are a lot of reason for pessimism, because we don't have strong governance setup at the state, national, and international levels. When the economy is doing well, people are talking about Climate Change but when the economy isn't doing well, it's not a popular topic.

It's hard to imagine what life looks like in Tacoma with sea level rise and waters rising like we discussed. What does that look like for someone living there in 2080?

I also think that people's ability to adapt to circumstances is incredible. Once it becomes clear that it's an apparent problem, we'll likely take appropriate actions to help. We don't need tons of new technology to solve this problem, just a will to act.

Summary

I think one of my biggest takeaways from this was how much people affect the environment around them and that scientist aren't just working on stabilizing Climate Change but are focused on how best to adapt to the changes that are happening now and into the future. Another key takeaway is that we as humans are quite adaptable to changes in our environment. It gives me hope that people like Dr. Guillaume are working on the problem.

CHAPTER EIGHT

DEFORESTATION, WILDFIRES, AND SOIL DEGRADATION

Did you know that tropical rainforests, which cover 6-7% of the Earth's surface, contain over half of all the plant and animal species in the world! In this chapter, we will be talking about deforestation, wildfires, and soil degradation, their causes, and their effect on the land and people. Each of these phenomena can affect not only the creatures and people, but the viability of areas to continue to sustain their ecosystems. Most of the concerning issues we're seeing are driven by human activity. Let's start with deforestation.

DEFORESTATION

As mentioned before, deforestation refers to the abrupt removal of ecosystems related to trees. The causes of deforestation take many forms: logging, mining, oil and gas extraction, cattle ranching, agriculture, and companies with little regard for the environment.

Logging is the action of cutting trees, and there are many methods to log. Two main methods to be exact! One of them is called Clear-cutting. Clear-cutting is the process of cutting a bunch of trees all at once. Another type of logging is simply the burning of trees. These methods were employed to turn forests into farmland. However, logging is destructive to the soils, wildlife, and atmosphere as there are less plants to absorb water and carbon dioxide. Trees retain water from their roots. So, if there aren't any trees to keep that water, there is a ton of excess water in the environment. This damages the low bearing plants, the animals that rely on those plants, and soil because of the water runoff—which muddies water and lowers the oxygen levels of the water ultimately harming aquatic life.

Other activities like mining, oil and gas extraction, cattle ranching, and agriculture encourage the destruction of forests and the wilderness. All these activities destroy the land through their preparation. Cattle ranching and agriculture can eradicate the wilderness through their aftermath while mining and oil and gas extraction cause deforestation along with many other problems.

Cattle ranching and agriculture have been the leading cause of deforestation in Central and South America because of the work needed to start the process of growing crops and raising cattle. To grow crops and raise cattle, farmers and cattle ranchers need open fields. In the rainforest, there aren't many plains and farmable land, so they have to make land through techniques of logging which leads to less trees in Central and South America and is the cause of two thirds of the deforestation in Brazil.

Other harmful activities affect the environment with their disastrous aftereffects: mining and oil and gas extraction. Mining and oil and gas extraction involves the clearing of trees, introduces pollutants, and disrupts the ecosystems balance with an increase of sediment which is pulled out of the ground when people mine. Like cattle ranching and agriculture, mining requires an open and flat piece of land which can be achieved through deforestation. Mining also releases pollutants into the environment which has repercussions for land and water living organisms. However, one of the most common negative effects originates from soil. When mining, there is a surplus of soil that must be removed to get to the good stuff, so miners dig up the dirt and plop in down in streams and other miscellaneous places in the environment. This increase of sediment can divert streams into other homes of cute baby wolves instead of the dens of furry beavers. Even though the thought of baby wolves in a swimming pool is super adorable, we must still stand strong, FOR THE BEAVERS!

All these activities revolve around deforestation and, even, lead to other problems that damage the surrounding ecosystem.

WILDFIRES

Wildfires (also called bushfires and forest fires) are fires that uncontrollably burn in natural areas like forests, grassland, or prairie. So, if there were a massive fire on Microsoft campus and it would not be considered a wildfire. That's just a fire and please call the proper authorities. Wildfires are dangerous because they spread quickly and can damage natural resources, destroy homes, and endanger nearby people and buildings.

Some causes are on accident or on purpose. Some accidental causes are by human or natural occurrences: dropped cigarettes, fireworks, flammable products, lightening, and lava. However, occasionally wildfires are started on purpose. This is called arson.

There are factors that can make wildfires spread quickly and become more dangerous: high winds and dry conditions. These small mistakes, like dropping a cigarette butt into dry grass, can lead to catastrophic effects.

To accidentally start fires, there must be a dry environment. Climate Change is a heavy contributor to the development of dangerous and wildfire prone environments by increasing the temperature in a place that was resistant to wildfires. In short, Climate Change worsens conditions by creating dangerous habitats that can harm the flora and fauna of the surrounding area through wildfires. To help stop wildfires and prepare the people affected, there are many organizations that help the environment and people. Specifically, in California and Australia because these areas are facing a hazardous number of wildfires.

SOIL DEGRADATION

If worldwide soil was a student, its grades would be dropping. As the name suggests, Soil degradation is the decline of soil quality caused by the effects of improper land use for agriculture, urban, or industrial purposes. Soil degradation affects the soil's physical, biological, and chemical state.

This problem arises in myriad ways. There are physical, biological, and chemical factors that cause soil degradation. The most prominent factors are wind and water erosion. Erosion is the process of wind or water breaking off rock, soil, or other dissolved materials and transporting them somewhere else. There also many ways that wind and water erosion can occur like rainfall, surface runoff, floods, tillage (preparing the ground for farming), and mass moments of Earth tend to result in the degradation of fertile topsoil and soil quality.

SUMMARY

Wildfires are increasing in frequency and intensity in many parts of the world. Helping control Climate Change and increasing responsible human activity will help fight these devastating forces of nature.

PLANET CROSSWORD PUZZLE

Across:

2. Contaminants in the air and water
3. Most common element in the atmosphere
6. Primary cause of Global Warming
7. The heating up of the planet
8. Clearing a wide area of forest

Down:

1. Created from the breakdown of organic material over millions of years
4. The unsustainable harvesting of fish
5. Primary greenhouse gas contributing to global warming

CHAPTER TEN

TECHNOLOGY, PEOPLE, AND HOPE

Although this book covers many areas of concern for the planet, I'm an optimist! I believe as a collective we have overcome and improved many large problems in the past, from reducing poverty to curing diseases to protecting the ozone layer. This chapter is to discuss all the great initiatives, technology, and progress made around these issues—I hope it inspires you to stay positive and get more involved.

POWER OF PEOPLE

Although we as people contribute to the problem, we have so much power to influence how companies and government behave around our planet. Recently, Microsoft announced an initiative for carbon footprint neutrality by 2030 and creating a carbon deficit by 2050. This is people power in the form of consumer demand.

Consumer Demand

Every time we buy something, we are making a statement about what we support. If we are just a little more conscious about whom we purchase from based that corporation's behavior, we have incredible power over the companies around us. In the Microsoft example above, if customers weren't demanding more responsibility from corporations, they wouldn't be taking initiatives like carbon neutrality. Wouldn't it be great if we could create some better visibility for consumers? What if when you bought a product, like a food label, we could read the Climate Change label as well.

Political Influence

Although many of us can't vote yet, when we become voting age, vote for people that represent the issues we care about. In the meantime, let's keep open lines of communication open with our parents to make sure they are voting responsibly as well.

INTERESTING TECHNOLOGY

Electric Cars

Electric cars are an important development for helping the planet. Hopefully in the future, electric cars truly become emissions free. Like I mentioned above, although Washington state produces 60% of its energy from green resources, we actually export much of that energy to other states and import a lot of coal energy from Montana. Since we charge our cars on the electrical grid, those cars are contributing to Montana carbon emissions unless we specifically say we want our energy at our house from renewable sources.

Electric cars are important though, not just to have vehicles with lower emissions, but it centralizes the energy problems with our energy agencies. So, as technology emerges to contain carbon emission and leverage more renewal sources, that technology can be applied centrally and benefit everyone on a very large scale quickly.

Companies like Carbon Engineering are working to pull Carbon Dioxide directly out of the air. I can imagine a day where regulations expect companies that burn fossil fuels to capture 99.9% of the carbon dioxide emissions they produce and responsibly dispose of the byproduct.

Carbon Engineering's Products (https://carbonengineering.com/).

Biodegradable Plastics

One of the big problems with plastics is how long they take to break down in the environment. Did you know it takes up to 450 years for a plastic bottle to break down?

Plastic was invented in 1907, so what this means is the majority of plastic that has been created in the last hundred years is still floating around in the environment.

Fortunately, there is a push to create Biodegradable Plastics. I know, big word, right? It just means that the plastic will naturally break down in the environment much more quickly. This is good for the environment, bad for my Lego set.

Biodegradable Plastics would reduce pollution and the amount of plastics and microplastics that make it into our bodies. Imagine if this was the technology from the beginning, there wouldn't be such a large patch of garbage in the Pacific Ocean and the stress on our marine life would be greatly reduced.

In 2019, Ohio State won awards for novel research that combined natural rubber and bioplastics to contain food. You ca read more about here: https://news.osu.edu/biodegradable-plastics-is-coolest-ohio-state-science-story-of-2019/

Solar Panels

Solar Panels are thin tiles that convert sun energy into electricity for us to use. When it comes to solar energy, there are challenges in terms of areas without a lot of sun, nighttime, and efficiency. One of the most interesting ones is efficiency. The more energy a panel can convert, the more people it can service and the less fossil fuels we need to burn.

Below is a graph of how solar panel efficiency has improved over time since 1975. Although the graph may be hard to read, it is clear that we're getting more efficient, which means we're getting closer and closer to solar panels augmenting more and more of our energy consumption.

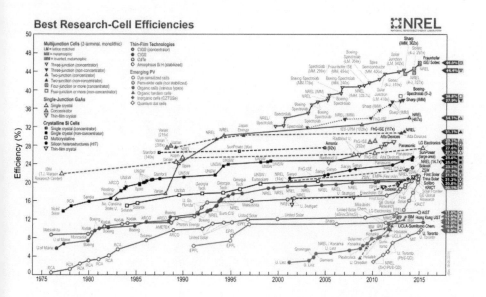

Not only is the technology getting better, but in the US, this is translating into more renewable energy capacity. You can see the trend below since 2005.

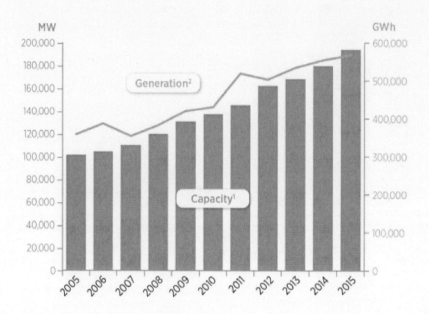

Summary

The main point is there are reasons to be hopeful and that as people, even as young adults and kids, we're not helpless to make an impact. There are plenty of things we can do to help.

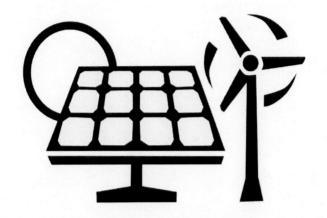

CHAPTER TWELVE

CONCLUSION

There are two key things I've learned about the choices we can make to help the environment. The first is that no choice is too small, every little bit helps if we just take action. I've also learned that one person isn't enough to protect the world, this is a collective effort, but one person can trigger changes by choosing to lead and speak up. The advancements in technology are exciting as well as people around the global continue to advocate to address issues like Climate Change.

Okay, I've thrown a lot of information at you, but the question is "how do I remember how to be a good stewardship of the planet?"

Well, always remember the established **Reduce, Reuse, and Recycle.** To remember what we've covered in this book, I have another trick to help you remember.

If you think about things that are hurting the planet, you can use the word **PLANET** as an acronym below:

P - Pollution

L - Land Use

A - Animal Products

N - New Purchases

E - Electricity

T - Transportation

POLLUTION refers to the contaminants released into our environment by corporations and people that cause damage to the planet, humans, and animals alike.

LAND USE refers deforestation and human activities that alter ecosystems.

ANIMAL PRODUCTS refers to the consumption of meat and it's impact on the environment. Eating more vegetables is good for you and reduces carbon emissions.

NEW PURCHASES refers to purchasing products from responsible companies that work to minimalize their impact on the environment.

ELECTRICITY refers to the use of energy, as it is the top cause of greenhouse gas emissions on the planet.

TRANSPORTATION refers to the use of cars and commercial vehicles. Biking and public transportation are much better options for our planet.

Thanks for taking the time to read my book and care about this place we call home. Remember, it's important to take an action, no matter how small, for us to make an accumulative effect.

Please share and recommend this book to others if you enjoyed it and it was helpful. We're also selling shirts on our website to help support and fund Climate Change initiatives. Bye and thank you so much for reading! Happy greenhouse gas hunting!

VISIT US AT:

https://kidshelpingtheplanet.com/

PLANET PRACTICAL HOME CHECKLIST
QUICK, PRINTABLE

- **FOLLOW** Reduce, Recycle, and Reuse

- **CONVERT** lights bulbs to energy efficient

- **ALWAYS** turn off electrical items when they are not in use

- **USE** public transportation or bike when possible

- **PURCHASE** from responsible corporations

- **REDUCE** the consumption of single-use plastics

- **EAT** more vegetables; less red meats, (it's good for you too!)

- **REMEMBER** electricity & transportation burn fossil fuels most

- **CONSIDER** supporting a Climate Change movement

- **ENJOY** vacationing locally

- **USE** rechargeable batteries

- **REMEMBER** things that hurt the **P-L-A-N-E-T**

  - P => POLLUTION

  - L => LAND USE

  - A => ANIMAL PRODUCTS

  - N => NEW PURCHASES

  - E => ELECTRICITY

  - T => TRANSPORTATION

* by Kid's Guide to Helping the Planet

CROSSWORD PUZZLE ANSWERS:

Get our Awesome Shirt and Help Support Stabilizing Climate Change

VISIT US AT:

https://kidshelpingtheplanet.com/

Appendix

GREAT RESOURCES FOR KIDS

Check out these great resources!

Kid's Guide to Helping the Planet
https://kidshelpingtheplanet.com/
Facebook: @kidsguideseries
Twitter: @kidsguideseries

World Health Organization
http://www.who.int/topics/environmental_health/factsheets/en/

NASA
https://climate.nasa.gov/causes/

Environmental Protection Agency
https://www.epa.gov/ghgemissions/sources-greenhouse-gas-emissions

National Geographic
https://www.youtube.com/watch?v=G4H1N_yXBiA

Made in United States
North Haven, CT
13 November 2021

11121331R00042